BIOLOGICAL WEAPONS – STILL A RELEVANT THREAT

Weapons of Mass Destruction (WMD) – Nuclear, Biological, and Chemical weapons - in the possession of hostile states and terrorists - represent one of the greatest security challenges facing the United States, and require a comprehensive strategy to counter them in all their dimensions.[1] The term Chemical, Biological, Radiological, Nuclear (CBRN) encompasses factors and effects these threats represent. The term CBRN originated during the cold war, but became commonly used, and interchangeable with WMD, after the terrorist attacks on American soil on September 11, 2001.

Disseminating CBRN weapons on a population will result in a wide variety of consequence management responses, depending on the type of weapon, level of extremity, and size of the affected area. The United States' National Security Strategy of 2002 addressed CBRN concerns at the strategic level. —The gravest danger our Nation faces lies at the crossroads of radicalism and technology. Our enemies have openly declared that they are seeking weapons of mass destruction, and evidence indicates that they are doing so with determination."[2] The recently published National Security Strategy of 2010 further articulated this concern, stating, —...This Administration has no greater responsibility than the safety and security of the American people. And there is no greater threat to the American people than weapons of mass destruction..."[3] This paper will discuss characteristics of CBRN threats, and why *one* of them poses a greater threat than the others - specifically biological weapons.

Time has diluted the concerns over the threat from biological weapons, as illustrated by the anthrax attacks in the autumn of 2001. However, biological agents remain relevant and evidence indicates that adversaries who wish us harm, have not lost their focus on weapons of mass destruction in general, and biological weapons in particular. The *IHS Janes: Defence and Security Intelligence & Analysis* website notes that a number of State actors possess not only one, but a combination of threats classified as CBRN. In addition, these State actors possess various delivery capabilities. The overall discussion outlines acquisition or possession of CBRN agents by both State and Non-state actors; level of difficulty in development and manufacture; observed and expected performance of the various agents in the environment; physiological effects on populations; and lastly, detection, identification, and containment requirements once an incident occurs.

It is important to differentiate between State actors and Non-state actors because State actors have more intrinsic capability and capacity to possess advanced CBRN programs, as well as advanced delivery capabilities. These capabilities will directly relate to the State actors' ability to attack a broader range of targets with wider range of strategic and operational effects. Non-state actors have far more limited options.

Additionally, the paper will present a risk assessment of CBRN agents as they relate to four specific factors of consequence management requirements within a CBRN response construct. This assessment will provide the necessary data to determine which of the CBRN agents pose the greatest threat.

The first factor is *speed of detection*. This is the time it takes to rapidly and accurately confirm the presence of an agent using current sensor detection technology. The ability to quickly detect an agent remains the first and vital step in the requirement to manage any CBRN hazard.

The second factor is *accuracy of identification*. This is the ability to correctly identify the specific CBRN agent present, using current agent identification technologies. The ability to accurately identify an agent is critical in countering the agent's effects.

The third factor is difficulty in *containing the contamination*. This measures the level of effort needed to contain the spread of the contamination. Once the presence of a CBRN agent is confirmed, the importance of limiting further exposure becomes critical.

The fourth factor is the level of difficulty in neutralizing or mitigating the effects of the agent. Rapidly neutralizing the effects of a CBRN agent is vitally important, not only because of the direct human physiological effects, but also because of the negative impact on government agencies' ability to restore and maintain order, while simultaneously meeting the need to provide basic services.

Table 1 will assist in identifying which CBRN agents pose the greatest threat. Each agent type (Chemical, Biological, or Nuclear) receives an assessment in terms of ―LOW", ―MEDIUM" or, ―HGH correlating to the risk associated with meeting the specific threat and consequence management requirements.

	Speed of Detection	Accuracy of Identification	Difficulty of Containment	Ability to Mitigate
Nuclear				
Chemical				
Biological				

Table-1: Risk Assessment Chart

As noted, the National Security Strategy, National Defense Strategy, and the National Military Strategy indicate the necessity of adequately addressing and mitigating CBRN threats. Further guidance is provided in the *National Strategy to Combat Weapons of Mass Destruction*, which states "An effective strategy for countering WMD, including their use and further proliferation, is an integral component of the National Security Strategy of the United States of America."[4] In order to execute an effective strategy to combat these threats, an understanding of the agents, their effects on the population, their methods of delivery, and their consequence management requirements is needed.

Nuclear Weapons

Overview and Background. Acquiring and possessing nuclear weapons is expensive and time-consuming. The infrastructure and manufacturing requirements needed to process the essential radioactive material, as well as the development and assembly of key components of a nuclear weapon is complex. This process demands a considerable amount of time, manpower, and funding. Currently, few State actors possess the requisite capability. The threat of *Non-state actors* having the ability to develop a nuclear weapon without assistance remains low. A General Accounting Office (GAO) report, *Observations on the Threat of Chemical and Biological Terrorism* stated, "...terrorists would have to overcome significant technical and operational challenges to successfully make and release chemical or biological agents...to kill or injure large numbers of people without substantial assistance from a State sponsor."[5]

When a nuclear explosion occurs, detection is immediate and unmistakable. The explosion produces tremendous heat and blast, and radiation. As described by R. Everett Langford, "While conventional explosives produce blast and heat, the amounts are minute compared to even the smallest nuclear weapon. The energy of a nuclear explosion is transferred to the surrounding medium in three distinct forms: blast; thermal radiation; and nuclear radiation."[6]

Historical pictures and first-hand accounts of the effects following the detonation of the atomic bombs at Hiroshima and Nagasaki in 1945, illustrate this point.

> A huge fireball formed in the sky. Together with the flash came the heat rays and blast, which instantly destroyed everything on earth and those in the area fell unconscious and were crushed to death. Then they were blown up in the air and hurled back to the ground. The roaring flames burned those caught under the structures that were crying or groaning for help.
>
> When the fire burnt itself out, there appeared a completely changed, vast, colorless world that made you think it was the end of life on earth. In a heap of ashes lay the debris of the disaster and charred trees, presenting a gruesome scene. The whole city became extinct. Citizens who were in Matsuyama Township, the hypocenter, were all killed instantly, excepting a child who was in an air-raid shelter.[7]

Figure 1: Hiroshima after Atomic Bomb Detonation

Figure-1 illustrates effects of the atomic bombs dropped on Hiroshima and Nagasaki. It is important to note that today's nuclear devices are thousands of times more powerful. Michael Kort writes, —The most powerful explosion was a Soviet test of a nuclear device in 1961. This explosion demonstrated the power and energy almost

5,000 times as powerful as the atomic bomb that destroyed the city of Hiroshima with of a force of 12 kilotons."[8]

As noted, the blast and heat effects of a nuclear weapon are immediate. The radiation effects occur later and have longer lasting implications. Beyond the immediate devastation, the detonation will result in significant devastation to populations and communities as radiation effects continue to manifest. Survivors will display thermal and radiation burns, as well as physiological effects from the radiation poisoning. Radiation symptoms include blisters, loss of hair, and cancer. Langford notes, "Some pre-natal infants, depending upon the time of exposure during development, will be born with birth defects, reduced mental abilities, or cancers."[9]

A nuclear incident will require immediate emergency management by police, fire and rescue, and medical authorities. The fact that the nature of the event is unmistakable, and immediately confirmable, will facilitate an immediate execution of response and mitigation procedures including radiation detection, containment, and decontamination.

Development and Delivery Methods. As noted, developing a nuclear weapon is resource intensive. The manpower and skills needed to monitor, manage, and control the processing of radioactive material into a viable nuclear weapon are intensive. Nuclear weapons can be categorized into those with crude designs and those with sophisticated designs. Crude designs still require detailed drawings and specifications before fabrication of a device occurs. Mark, Taylor, et al, address this reality with respect to whether terrorists can actually reach the nuclear threshold:

> The preparation of these drawings requires a large number of man-hours and the direct participation of individuals with specific skills in several quite

distinct areas, such as in the physical, chemical, and metallurgical properties of the various materials to be used, as well as the characteristics affecting their fabrication; neutronic properties; radiation effects, both nuclear and biological; technology concerning high explosives and/or chemical propellants; some hydrodynamics; electrical circuitry; and others.[10]

There are various methods to deliver a nuclear weapon that are largely determined by the strategic or tactical objective of the State or Non-state actor using the weapon, as well as by the means available. Sophisticated delivery systems are expensive to develop or acquire, and exploiting the necessary technology leaves a trail, revealing the actor's intent and capability.

Seeking a strategic objective, State actors would more than likely use long-range ballistic missiles or long-range strategic bombers should they have that capability. Ballistic missiles and strategic bombers provide greater accuracy in targeting specific locations, such as command and control buildings, financial centers, logistical hubs, and supply areas, as well as densely populated areas. Targeting these strategic objectives serves to destroy the capacity of an adversary to wage war. Due to the magnitude of the detonation this would require, such an objective requires a weapon with a high explosive yield, demanding the stand-off advantages of ballistic missiles or long-range bombers.

Seeking a tactical objective, State actors would more than likely use artillery, smaller aircraft, or short-range missiles. The reduced size of the specific targets directly correlates to the smaller coverage area as well as a lower yielded detonation required to achieve the desired tactical effects.

If a Non-state actor were to attempt to acquire and deliver a nuclear weapon, the difficulties in acquiring the needed materials would certainly drive them toward a smaller weapon, more on the scale of a tactical weapon. Delivery would likely be through covert means, such as a shipping container. Their ultimate aim is to instill fear, and terror, while simultaneously attempting to make a political, religious, or ideological point.

Chemical Weapons

Overview and Background. The requirements to develop chemical capable weapons range from very simple to highly complex. The skills and resources needed to build infrastructure, and acquire and manufacture chemical agents are arguably available in most moderately industrialized States.

A chemical weapon is defined by the Organisation for the Prohibition of Chemical Weapons (OPCW) as a toxic chemical contained in a delivery system, such as a bomb or shell.[11] The term, chemical weapon, includes toxic chemicals or precursors that cause death, injury, temporary incapacitation or sensory irritation through its chemical action. Munitions or other devices designed to deliver chemical weapons, whether filled or unfilled, are also considered weapons themselves. Chemical weapons are categorized as choking, blister, blood, or nerve agents. According to the OPCW, —fte most well-known agents are...: choking agents - chlorine and phosgene, blister agents (or vesicants) - mustard and lewisite, blood agents - hydrogen cyanide, nerve agents - sarin, soman, VX."[12]

The *type* of chemical agent will determine the specific human physiological effects. In general, the physiological effect depends on the type of agent used, but includes coughing, choking, muscle spasm, blisters, and convulsions. The surrounding physical environment can impact the effects of these agents. Humidity, rain-fall, wind, and bright sunlight can weaken the effects and persistency of the chemical agents.

Winds can also send the agent in the wrong direction or even back onto the troops who released it.

Persistent agents typically remain present in the affected area for longer periods of time--hours to days-- and, depending on the environment and agent, can last for weeks. An example of a persistent agent is a blister agent. These agents are typically used to deny access to a particular area or terrain, channelize an attacking force, contaminate material, and disrupt, injure or incapacitate the enemy.

Non-persistent agents typically remain present in the affected area for shorter periods of time--seconds to minutes--and, depending on the environment and agent, can last for hours. An example of a non-persistent agent is a blood or choking agent. These agents are typically used to temporarily disrupt, immobilize, degrade the performance of and/or hinder the activities of the enemy for a period of time. This disruption will typically allow an attacking force to go on the offensive and successfully seize key terrain previously occupied by the enemy.

The spectrum of chemical agents range from non-lethal incapacitants, such as Tear Gas to highly lethal organophosphates agents such as nerve agents. Nerve agents, by far, are the most lethal agents. They are odorless and colorless with death occurring within seconds. The physiological effects of nerve agents consist of contraction of pupils, profuse salivation, convulsions, involuntary urination and defecation.

World War I saw the first and most widespread use of chemical agents. Both sides used choking as well as blister agents during the conflict. Although popular belief suggests the German army was the first to use gas, it was in fact initially deployed by the French. In the first month of the war, August 1914, French troops fired tear-gas grenades against the Germans.[13] A more recent example is Saddam Hussein's use of chemical weapons on the Kurdish town of Halabja in 1988.[14]

Figure-2 depicts a human arm exposed to a blister agent. Blister agents, such as mustard gas, are in the chemical agent category that exhibit the greatest persistence in the environment.[15]

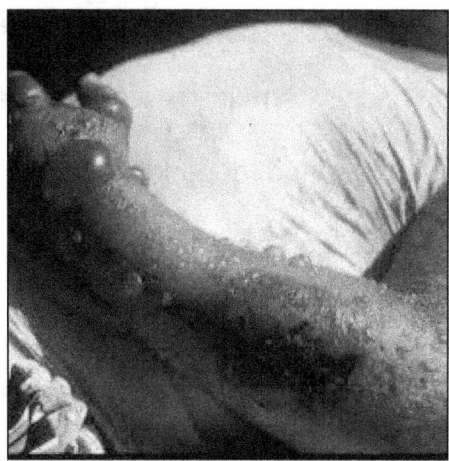

Figure 2: Human Arm Exposed to a Blister Agent

Confirmation as to whether a chemical attack occurred would be nearly immediate. Clinical signs would also indicate the class of chemical agent. This is important for the rapid initiation of consequence management procedures including decontamination and contamination containment. At very low levels of contaminations, the capability exists to accurately detect and identify these hazards.

Development and Delivery Methods. Developing chemical weapons requires proper and constant monitoring and spans a spectrum of complexity, from relatively simple to highly complex. An example of a relatively simple agent would be a ubiquitous poison such as cyanide. A toxic and deadly substance, cyanide has been used as a poison for thousands of years. The effects of a high dose of cyanide are quick, and death occurs within minutes.

There are a variety of likely delivery methods for chemical weapons, which will be determined by the strategic or tactical effects that State or Non-state actors wish to achieve. With a strategic objective in mind, State actors will likely use persistent agents to contaminate and deny use of key locales. Due to the depth in the battle-space where these strategic targets reside, as well as the intent to avoid them, a wide variety of delivery systems such as ballistic and cruise missiles, air assets, and even large scale artillery pieces can be used to deliver these types of agents. With a tactical objective in mind, State actors will more than likely use non-persistent agents to attack fielded forces and seize terrain. Delivery may be through artillery or aircraft. Non-state actors may have the ability to employ persistent or non-persistent agents, but are likely limited in their ability to affect a wide area because they would have limited quantities. This limitation confines them to more tactical or terror-producing objectives.

Biological Weapons

Overview and Background. The materials and technology needed to develop and manufacture biological agents also range from very simple to complex. The likelihood of a State actor obtaining and possessing a biological warfare capability remains highly relevant, partly because the processes used in developing biological agents are also found in such innocuous endeavors as pharmaceutical and vaccine production. Arguably, the removal, or addition of a step within a vaccine manufacturing process can serve as a source of a biological weapon. One of the issues which cause concern with biological agents is the time required to detect and confirm that an incident occurred.

Cellular or molecular life sciences defines biological agents, or bioterrorism as, —the intentional or threatened use of microorganisms or toxins derived from living organisms to cause death or diseases in humans, animals or plants on which we depend."[16] Common symptoms of a biological attack may include fever, coughing, headache, muscle or joint pain, sore throat, chills, fatigue, and running nose. These are not only symptoms from a potential biological agent attack, but represent symptoms of the flu or common cold. One of the many challenges therefore with biological agents is differentiating between an actual *biological attack* and common illnesses.

In 2001 Anthrax-tainted letters sent through the Post office, killed five and infected twenty-two people. While the number of casualties was low, the ensuing panic shut down postal delivery across the country and reinforced fears raised by Al Qaeda's attacks in New York City and Washington DC. In the climate stemming from those attacks, United States policy makers considered nation-wide smallpox vaccinations to preempt a terrorist use of smallpox. The effects of smallpox after the on-set of symptoms are illustrated in Figure – 3.[17]

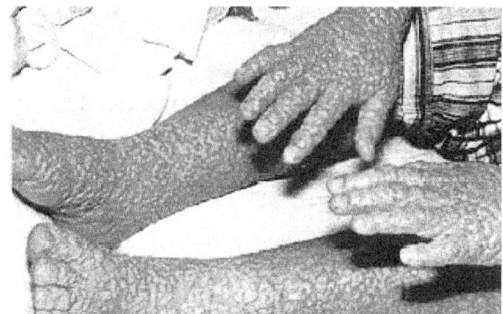

Figure 3: Human Infected with Smallpox Virus

Human physiological effects and the symptoms of a biological attack remain difficult to rapidly detect. The incubation period of a particular agent may take anywhere from two to forty days (depending on the concentration and type of agent).[18] This will occur prior to the infected person beginning to exhibit symptoms. As stated in the journal BioTechniques —...biological warfare agents are the most problematic of the weapons of mass destruction and terror. Both civilian and military sources predict that over the next decade the threat from proliferation of these agents will increase significantly."[19]

Development and Delivery Methods. Developing a biological weapon can range from very simple to very complex. At the simple end of the spectrum, any form of microbiological contamination that disrupts the health of a target population could serve as a biological weapon. Because much of the material and equipment used to produce biological weapons has legitimate medical, agricultural, or commercial purposes, and because production of biological agents could occur covertly in a relatively small facility, nations or groups could acquire clandestine biological weapons programs. As previously stated, the addition, or elimination of a manufacturing processing step within a pre-existing vaccination production facility can potentially create a biological weapon. On the complex end of the spectrum, State actors would sponsor genetic engineering of bacteria or viruses to produce super strains or highly viable and infectious bio-organisms.

Delivery systems for biological agents may vary from missiles for strategic targets to the use of small injectors for individual targets; as in the case of Georgi Markov, a Bulgarian dissident assassinated by the Bulgarian secret police in 1978.[20] If more surreptitious methods are used, dissemination will more than likely go unnoticed, which further exacerbates the problem of managing effects of a biological weapon.

13

Once biological agents are released in the environment, predicting their behavior and duration of viability may be difficult. If the agents survive the delivery mechanism, which in the case of missile or bomblet delivery involves low yield explosions for airborne dispersal, the agents' viability may also be affected by natural phenomena such as sunlight, temperatures, or humidity. "[21]

The term —iability," with respect to a biological organism, means that the organism has the ability to live in the environment, replicate, and remain infectious. However, biological agents need not be transmissible; anthrax is viable, but does not replicate, at least not in the form that would be used in an attack, and it is not transmissible from human to human. Indeed, anthrax's lack of transmissibility contributes to its likely value as a biological agent in that its effects are more controllable than that of agents that are transmissible once fielded. If a biological agent, such as smallpox, is transmissible once it is fielded, then managing—and identifying--infected persons can be very difficult. Further, biological agents may be disseminated in much higher dosages than would naturally occur, and through atypical transmission routes. This factor will help defeat counter-measures that are based on the way these organisms would behave under natural circumstances. During the agent's incubation period (the time between infection and display of clinical signs and symptoms), the infected persons may be able to further—and widely—disseminate the agent.

Consequence Management and Response

Once a CBRN attack occurs, proper authorities must initiate an effective consequence management strategy. The strategy must take into account all actions necessary to limit further loss of life, ensure protection of property and infrastructure, maintain order, and restore any interrupted essential services. Further, they must take

14

appropriate steps to reduce the effects of the incident by limiting and/or isolating the contaminated area in addition to the requirements to plan, prepare, coordinate, and provide effective care and management to infected personnel. Nuclear, chemical, and biological agents present different levels of complexity in successfully designing a viable response and containment strategy.

Nuclear Agents. As a reminder, indications of a nuclear detonation will be immediate. The bright flash, the widespread physical destruction, the searing heat, and the mushroom cloud will provide immediate evidence that a nuclear incident occurred. Visible consequences of radiation are unlikely. Once heat and blast casualties are addressed, the focus of the response must shift to the detection and identification of radiological contamination. Many instruments currently exist which effectively measure the presence of radiological contamination. These instruments detect very low levels of contamination, as well as determine the type of radiological material with great accuracy. These detectors facilitate monitoring and surveying for, and containment of, contamination from radioactive material. First responders in some areas and most hazmat units are equipped with detectors and could confirm a radioactive release associated with an explosion soon after arrival on the scene."[22] Once the outside limits of the contamination are identified, then rapid execution of decontamination can occur. Individuals should minimize contact of radioactive material with skin and eyes by rinsing exposed skin, removing contact lenses, and showering as soon as possible."[23]

Referring back to Table 1; the factors of *speed of detection*; *accuracy of identification*; *difficulty to contain*; and *ability to mitigate* are assessed as a —LOW" risk for nuclear agents

Chemical Agents. A chemical attack is the deliberate release of a toxic gas, liquid, or solid which poisons people and the environment. Odors and clouds of gas may or may not be evident. As discussed, nerve agents, which are odorless and colorless, represent one of the most toxic chemical agents. Langford states, ―Nerve agents will cause tightness in the chest, salivation, and pulmonary edema with possible shaking, sweating and loss of bodily functions."[24]

Current technology allows rapid detection of attack and verification of the presence of most known chemical agents, as well as the ability to accurately identify the agent. These technologies range in cost and in complexity. At the low cost, simple design end of the spectrum, ―M8 and M9 Detection Papers", used by the US Army and Marine Corps are an example of this capability. These papers quickly and easily detect the presence of Nerve and Blister agents. At the other end of the high cost, complex design end of the spectrum, the military uses the M21 Remote Sensing Chemical Agent Alarm (RSCAAL). This technology offers a long range, stand-off capability to detect the presence of nerve and blister agents up to 5,000 meters away.[25]

As a reminder, chemical agents can be categorized into two general types– persistent, and non-persistent. Persistent agents represent a *contact hazard*, which means an individual must physically come in contact with the agent in order to be infected. Persistent agents last from anywhere from hours to days in the environment. Non-persistent agents represent an *inhalation or absorption hazard*, which typically means an individual, must inhale the agent or absorb it through the skin in order to be affected. Non-persistent agents can last anywhere from minutes to hours in the environment.

With this being the case, the effort needed to contain the spread of the contamination remains manageable. Depending on the type of agent, proven therapeutics exists, including antidotes, and compounds that successfully counter or mitigates the effects of exposure. ―Decontamination of chemically contaminated patients typically requires the removal of their clothing and the use of a variety of decontamination kits and solutions..."[26]

Referring back to Table 1, the factors of *speed of detection*, *accuracy of identification*, *difficulty to contain*, and *ability to mitigate* are assessed as a ―LOW" risk for chemical agents.

Biological Agents. A biological attack is the deliberate release of bacteria, viruses, rickettsia, or toxins, or other biological substances which cause illness. ―Some biological agents, such as anthrax, do not cause contagious diseases. Others, like the smallpox virus, can result in disease you can catch from other people. Unlike an explosion, a biological attack may or may not be immediately obvious."[27]

A biological attack may go unnoticed within an area for several days or even weeks, depending on incubation periods. Therefore the detection and containment aspects of consequence management will likely be delayed. Some biological agents, particularly anthrax spores, have the potential to survive in the environment for extended periods of time, causing further risk of exposure and infection.

If detection of a biological attack occurs simultaneously with or immediately after a release, consequence management personnel can take rapid action to prevent further exposure and infection (moving away from and cordoning off the release area as well as instituting early prophylaxis). At this point, however, an attack is likely to be detected only after those who are initially infected present symptoms and/or report to health care facilities and is diagnosed with the disease.[28]

Current technology exists that allows rapid detection of the presence of a biological agent. The process of actually identifying *which* agent will take slightly longer to achieve. Field analytics lack the ability to perform positive confirmatory identification of a potential biological agent. That process is still confined to the laboratory environment and remains relatively complex, both in time and resources.

Depending on the biological agent, a variety of proven therapeutics exists, including antibiotics, vaccines, and antitoxins, which will mitigate the effects of a biological agent exposure. The sooner the attack is recognized and the agent and routes of infection identified, therapeutic intervention can be initiated.

United States defense officials continue to research and develop more user- and environmentally-friendly biological agent decontaminants. The use of soap and water to wash hands and other body parts exposed to the agent [remain] the quickest and best" solutions.[29]

Referring back to Table 1, the factors of *speed of detection*; *accuracy of identification*; and *difficulty to contain* area assessed as a ―HIGH" risk for biological agents. The *ability to mitigate* also is assessed as a ―HIGHrisk, until identification of the type of agent occurs, and then the factor is assessed as ―LOW".

Table 1 presented four factors for consideration in assessing risk in relation to consequence management of CBRN incidents. The preceding analysis provides the data point's needed to populate the matrix. Each column provides the risk assessment for each agent as they correlate to the specific consequence management factors.

Based on this data, biological weapons pose the greatest threat. Table 2 illustrates these findings:

	Speed of Detection	Accuracy of Identification	Difficulty of Containment	Ability to Mitigate
Nuclear	LOW	LOW	LOW	LOW
Chemical	LOW	LOW	LOW	LOW
Biological	HIGH	HIGH	HIGH	HIGH-LOW

Table-2: Risk Assessment Chart (with Data)

Non-State Actors and CBRN

With respect to attacks from Non-state actors, it is important to highlight the "R" within the CBRN lexicon. This —Rrepresents radioactive debris dispersed by a convention high explosive. Radiological Dispersal Devices (RDDs), or —dirty bombs" are a concern within the CBRN defense community, and would likely be used by Non-state actors. The actual radiological danger from RDDs is relatively low. Their primary danger is from the high-explosive used to propel the radiological debris. They are principally intended to sow terror.

Although studies suggest Non-state actors and terrorist groups remain vigilant in their efforts to obtain CBRN capabilities, their lack of resources limits their ability to procure nuclear weapons or the means to produce large quantities of chemical or biological agents. Further, their limited capacity to deliver CBRN agents will restrict potential employment opportunities to more localized areas. —AQaeda has a history of being interested in CBRN weapons and recent events, including the apparent disappearance of its known CBRN experts, indicate a renewed focus with particular regard to nuclear and biological attacks."[30]

Terrorist groups organize attacks in order to maximize their terror value. Crowded locations such as train stations and airports would provide excellent target opportunity's for CBRN attacks. Typically, terrorists use human beings as their delivery systems, rather than rockets or bombs. Ultimately, these attacks create fear and terror while having some capability to further distribute contaminants in the ensuing panic following the initial attack.[31]

The effort by the Aum Shinrikyo terrorist group provides an example of a CBRN terrorist attack. In 1995 they (Aum Shinrikyo) carried out a chemical attack on the Tokyo subway system. They released sarin gas within the train cars. Amy Zalman writes, ―The gas had been placed on trains in liquid form, in bottles disguised as drink bottles, and in other similarly disguised packaging. Gas was released when the packages leaked."[32] This particular attack killed twelve and affected an estimated six thousand people who were in the affected subway stations.

Conclusion

This paper provides an overview of the various agents which comprise CBRN, and discusses the differing capabilities of State and Non-state actors. State actors possess the ability to acquire and manufacture large quantities of CBRN agents. They possess the ability to develop and deliver CBRN agents across a spectrum of strategic and tactical objectives. Non-state actors possess a limited ability to acquire and manufacture CBRN agents. They lack the capability to develop and deliver CBRN agents on any large scale, and are therefore limited to small area coverage resulting in more tactical type effects. They may garner assistance from some State actors to accomplish their objectives.

The agents' physiological effects were assessed, along with the requirements and difficulties of detection, identification, and containment. Based on that assessment, biological agents represent the greatest threat because of:

- The delay in detecting a biological event - caused by the difficulty to determine the difference between an actual attack, or a naturally occurring illness;

- The delay in accurately identifying the particular agent; caused by the delay in detecting the biological attack, compounded by current technological limitations in positively confirming the type of agent;

- The difficulty in the containing the contamination caused by the delay in the detection and identification of the attack, as well as the resulting incubation period; and

- The ability to quickly mitigate the effects of biological agent exposure - caused by the length of time it takes to detect, and positively identify the type of agent.

As described by the Rapid Detection and Identification of Infectious Disease Agents, —Biological Warfare Agents (BWAs)…are the most problematic of the weapons of mass destruction…BWAs could kill more people than a nuclear or chemical attack."[33]

It is necessary to recognize from whom, and where, the threat will come. Biological agents can be unreliable once released in the environment. Because of this, State-actor's will, for the most part, commit more of their resources to developing nuclear and chemical weapons, which behave more predictably in the environment.

The potential for a biological attack will more than likely come from a Non-state actor or terrorist group. Biological weapons and potential delivery capabilities are well within the means of even small, poorly funded groups. The weapons can be acquired or developed in amounts and levels of complexity (or simplicity) that makes them an excellent choice for limited targets with the maximum yield of terror. Because their focus is to incite as much terror as possible, any potential attacks would likely be concentrated in population centers.

What is the right balance in providing necessary information about potential threats to hospitals, clinics, public health centers and first responders (including police, firefighters and emergency medical personnel)? While keeping responsible parties informed is important, caution is also important. As groups prepare for a potential biological attack, minimizing public panic is critical. Initially, public panic may cause misinformed households to take unnecessary—and possibly harmful—measures in response to a perceived attack. They may hoard antibiotics, and worse, self-prescribe counter-measures for themselves and their families that are dangerous or render counter-measures unavailable when truly needed. Moreover, over time, the public may begin to ignore, or downplay emergency notifications when an actual threat of attack becomes imminent.

Finally, we need to remain vigilant. Just because the last, arguably successful, biological attack occurred on our soil in 2001, doesn't mean the problem has gone away. The threat is still there and there needs to be a comprehensive Biological Surveillance program that brings disparate capabilities together; capabilities that facilitate effectively and efficiently connecting medical treatment and vaccine protocol programs, sensor technology developments, first responder capabilities, and intelligence agency inputs. There needs, as well, to be continued research and development of sensor technologies, which serve as the first line of warning for a potential biological attack. Sensor development needs to remain in step with the rapidly changing and different strands, mutations, and —threats of the day" which may evolve over time. Prophylaxis and therapeutic protocols need to reviewed and updated as needed.

Most importantly, increased cross agency-coordination—across all levels of government (federal, state, and local)—must be ensured. This cross-agency coordination can be in the form of information sharing, collaborative exercises, and interagency temporary assignments. These efforts will strengthen our concerted biological defense efforts.

Endnotes

[1] National Strategy to Combat of Weapons of Mass Destruction (December 2002), 1

[2] Ibid, 1

[3] National Security Strategy (May 2010), 4

[4] National Strategy to Combat of Weapons of Mass Destruction (December 2002), 1

[5] U.S. General Accounting Office, Combating Terrorism: Observations on the Threat of Chemical and Biological Terrorism, GAO/T-NSIAD-00-50, (Washington D.C.: U.S. Government Accountability Office, 1999).

[6] R. Everett Langford, —Introduction to Weapons of Mass Destruction – Radiological, Chemical and Biological," John Wiley and Sons, Inc., Hoboken, New Jersey 2004, 98

[7] Photograph with accompanying narrative of Hiroshima and Nagasaki immediately after the detonation of the Atomic bomb; available from http://www.gensuikin.org/english/ photo.html; internet accessed 10 January 2012

[8] Michael Kort, ─Weapons of Mass Destruction", Infobase publishing 2010, New York, New York 10001, 16

[9] R. Everett Langford, ─Introduction to Weapons of Mass Destruction – Radiological, Chemical and Biological," 109

[10] Mark, J. Carson; Taylor, Theodore; Eyster, Eugene; Maraman, William; Wechsler, Jacob ─Can Terrorists Build Nuclear Weapons?", Nuclear Control Institute, Washington DC, http://www.nci.org/k-m/makeab.htm; internet accessed 26 January 2012

[11] Organisation for the Prohibition of Chemical Weapons; available from http://www.opcw.org/about-chemical-weapons/what-is-a-chemical-weapon/; internet accessed 20 January 2012

[12] Ibid

[13] A multimedia history of world war one; available from http://www.firstworldwar.com/weaponry/gas.htm; internet accessed 3 March 2012

[14] 1988: The Halabja Massacre; available from http://libcom.org/history/1988-the-halabja-massacre; internet accessed 3 March 2012

[15] Photograph of Chemical Agent effects; available from http://www.google.com/search?q=saddam+hussein+chemical+weapons+kurds&hl=en&rlz=1R2TSNJ_enUS441&prmd=imvnso&source=lnms&tbm=isch&ei=ciMUT-fsMIHz0gHjrvWTAw&sa=X&oi=mode_link&ct=mode&cd=2&sqi=2&ved=0CAwQ_AUoAQ&biw=1366&bih=526#tbnh=162&tbnw=216&hl=en&rlz=1R2TSNJ_enUS441&sig=113444349287216898805&tbm=isch&sa=1&q=blister+agent+symptoms&oq=blister+agent&aq=2S&aqi=g2g-S6g-mS2&aql=&gs_sm=e&gs_upl=225025l227921l0l231223l13l12l0l1l1l0l203l1195l6.4.1l11l0&bav=on.2,or.r_gc.r_pw.r_qf.,cf.osb&fp=ac0cf6710d43ee95&biw=1366&bih=526; internet accessed 14 January 2012

[16] Bossi, P., Garin, D., Guihot, A., Gay, F., Crance, J. -., Debord, T., . . . Bricaire, F. (2006). Biological weapons. *Cellular and Molecular Life Sciences, 63*(19-20), 2196-2212. doi:10.1007/s00018-006-6308-z; available from http://search.proquest.com/docview/346839882/fulltextPDF?accountid=4444; internet accessed 5 March 2012

[17] www2a.cdc.gov

[18] Bossi, P., Garin, D., Guihot, A., Gay, F., Crance, J. -., Debord, T., . . . Bricaire, F. (2006). Biological weapons. *Cellular and Molecular Life Sciences, 63*(19-20), 2196-2212. doi:10.1007/s00018-006-6308-z; available from http://search.proquest.com/docview/346839882/fulltextPDF?accountid=4444; internet accessed 5 March 2012

[19] Dmitri Ivnitski1, Daniel J. O'Neil2, Anthony Gattuso3, Roger Schlicht3, Michael Calidonna4, and Rodney Fisher4, ─Nucleic acid approaches for detection and identification of biological warfare and infectious disease agents" RAPID DETECTION AND IDENTIFICATION OF INFECTIOUS DISEASE AGENTS, BioTechniques 35:862-869 (October 2003); HTTP://WWW.GMO-QPCR-ANALYSIS.COM/IVNITSKI-2003.PDF internet accessed 28 January 2012

[20] Secrets of the Dead, available from http://www.pbs.org/wnet/secrets/previous_seasons/case_umbrella/index.html; internet accessed 13 March 2012

[21] R. Everett Langford, "Introduction to Weapons of Mass Destruction – Radiological, Chemical and Biological," 200

[22] Davis, Lynn E, LaTourrette, T., Mosher, David E., Davis, Louis M., Howell, David R., "Individual Preparedness and Response to Chemical, Radiological, Nuclear, and Biological Terrorist Attacks (RAND Publishing) Arlington, VA 2003, 31

[23] Ibid, 42

[24] R. Everett Langford, "Introduction to Weapons of Mass Destruction – Radiological, Chemical and Biological,", 318

[25] Ibid, 294

[26] Ibid, 306

[27] Ibid, 317

[28] Davis, Lynn E, LaTourrette, T., Mosher, David E., Davis, Louis M., Howell, David R., "Individual Preparedness and Response to Chemical, Radiological, Nuclear, and Biological Terrorist Attacks (RAND Publishing) Arlington, VA 2003, 44

[29] Ibid, 44

[30] IHS Janes: Defence and Security Intelligence & Analysis; available from http://jcbrn.janes.com.ezproxy.usawcpubs.org/JDIC/JCBRN/home.do; internet accessed 4 February 2012

[31] Ibid

[32] Amy Zalman, Ph.D., 1995: Aum Shinrikyo Tokyo Subway Gas Attack Terrorist Attack Profile: Chemical Terrorism, Religious Terrorism, About.com Guide; available from http://terrorism.about.com/od/originshistory/a/AumShinrikyo.htm; internet accessed 6 March 2012

[33] Dmitri Ivnitski1, Daniel J. O'Neil2, Anthony Gattuso3, Roger Schlicht3, Michael Calidonna4, and Rodney Fisher4, "Nucleic acid approaches for detection and identification of biological warfare and infectious disease agents" RAPID DETECTION AND IDENTIFICATION OF INFECTIOUS DISEASE AGENTS, BioTechniques 35:862-869 (October 2003); HTTP://WWW.GMO-QPCR-ANALYSIS.COM/IVNITSKI-2003.PDF internet accessed 28 January 2012

www.ingramcontent.com/pod-product-compliance
Lightning Source LLC
Chambersburg PA
CBHW081811280526
45789CB00008B/3093